EROTIKA HOT STORIES - Part 3:

from the depth of the woman's mysterious soul **overwhelmed with passionate desires**

for men

and

for curious women

(Large Print Edition)

by

Diane Rausch

EROTIKA HOT STORIES - PART 3:
Overwhelmed with Passionate Desires

Stories

Be Ready to Have Me Good, My Captain

What am I going to do with you, my dearest?

I am smiling because whatever I will do will bring a lot of pleasure to both of us.

It is raining cats and dogs behind the window as I am writing this to be together with you for the few moments when you read it. I am together with you almost all the time now. I woke up in the morning and the first thought is about you. When I know you are thinking about me too, or I hear your voice, my heart starts beating faster. Is "beating" not very correct word for the "heart"? I know "pounding" and the other word I do not remember now. Maybe it is "palpitating"? The latter sounds very "medical" though. I like "beating" better. I love my heart beating for you.

I am shaking my knee in anticipation now when writing this and bringing up in my head the image of you sitting and looking at me. I am getting excited. I love your gray eyes. They got me once: now I think that it is forever.

For some reason I only imagine you in blue jeans. That is the only image I have in my head. However, the image is strong. It never goes away anymore. I am thinking about you almost all the time, day and night, with the exceptions when my mind is turned to the work I have to do or necessary chores and duties.

Now I am hugging you and kissing you, in a very wet way, and very long. I love your lips, they are very cute for kissing. I run the tip of my tongue over your lips and I touch the tip of your tongue. It is a very delicious feeling. My hand goes down in a natural   direction towards   your   thing, feels it, and fondles it through the jeans.

Your thing is hard and   warm.   My   hand unzips the jeans that are on the way to the trophy,   the   sweet trophy,   the   desirable destination of my love. I am   lowering   my   head helping get it out to the world with my lips.

I kiss it very tenderly. Now I got it out entirely. It is very cute and I love to caress it, because I think it loves it very much too. I am kissing it and going down along it with the tip of my tongue from the top to the base on one side; then I take it into the mouth and tenderly push it deeper.

You are having now a warm and pleasant feeling of being in the paradise with the woman who you always want.

I take your cute cock out now, slowly and tenderly, and I run my tongue on the other side of it from top to the base. I am taking it inside my mouth again. And I am performing the movement in and out, in and out, in and out. I try to go as deep as I can. I try to give you a pleasure with all the love I have for you. It is a lot of love, and it is a lot of pleasure.

I am sucking it now. It is very delicious. It is

my Captain. My pussy is squeezing now from desire when I am writing this. It is my beloved. It is My Love sitting in front of me. I want a part of him inside me. I need it as a fuel to continue living. I love you so much. I cannot live without you anymore.

I am taking your thing out and inviting you on the top of me. We are fondling my pussy. It is warm outside and wet inside when you go inside the pink lips, the tender curtains, and it is waiting patiently, with all its pussy's soul, eager to take part in the magic action of the two loving people. While waiting it is making contractions, like it has the heart of its own that is pounding. It is a separate entity now. It has the mind of its own, the same as your cock.

My pussy loves your cock very much. It wants to be united with your hard stiff tender cock as often as it can.

It is a beautiful thing what we are going to do now. The reunion of our eager sexual parts is about to happen.

I direct your hard cock into my eager soft pussy. You are doing me from the top now. I am dying under you from happiness. I am moving together with you. I am saying, "My

Captain, I love you so much. Tell me that you love me. Faster, faster. Go stronger, my beloved Captain." We do it very passionately and excitingly until you ready to finish.

I am asking you where you want to finish. You never want to tell me. OK. Then, let's finish in the mouth. I want to have a part of you in me. Let the taste of it remind me of you and your presence in me at least a minute longer. Every minute spent with you is very precious to me. It is the minute of happiness. Happiness bigger than this world, happiness out of this world.

I love you so much.

We rest and smile, and laugh: we are very happy. You fondle me, and I fondle you. I got you hard the second time. You lick me some, and then we fuck again. We fuck hard and tender. So much love, it is even unbearable to tolerate, if I may say so. There is no end of this desire for pleasure of having each other. There is only natural physical exhaustion that can separate us for a while of rest.

I love you, love you, love you.

Thank you for instilling in me so much love. I am not made of steel, like you, my beloved; I am going to the bathroom to my water arrangement. I need to act on this nice sharing of mine. When I finish, the action of the loving reunion with you will be completed for me.

I want and I hope that reading my words will make you unbearably aroused. I know that you know how to please me and that you would enjoy doing so. You are saying that I am a very sensual woman. Yes! For you!

You are saying that I am a totally delightful sexual being. You are saying to me that you desire me so much it is almost painful...

I Want to Finish to Release the Tension

Ok, my Baby.

Now, that I have done my urgent chores, I can relax with my beloved Baby.

I feel sexually anxious because I did not sleep well almost for the entire week, just was very busy, and this is how body reacts to this exhaustion, I noticed.

Tomorrow I have to go to work, but now I want just to go and lie down with a book, and fall asleep.

However, before that I want to finish in order to release the physical tension inside me of over-exhaustion for the week.

I could go to the bedroom and do it with myself there thinking of you.

But I do not want to because I want to show my Baby different picture. I want my dear Baby be very well entertained. Hopefully it will help him to forget about his current preoccupations.

OK, I will write this, and then I will go to the shower and do exactly, as I write. So, if you read it a few times or slowly, we actually will be doing it together. What a luxurious feeling and thought! I did it many times through my life. I told you that in my previous marriage my sexual drive was stronger than my husband's, so I had to do my self-relaxation sessions from time to time. I did different things with myself, but they will be exposed to you in due order.

I am going to do it now in the bathtub.

I am filling the bathtub with a somewhat hot water not to freeze there.

Now I am making the current of water from the showerhead not too weak (it is flexible, you know movable around, not adjusted over the head of the person), and not too strong. The water should go not too weak and not too strong. Not too hot, but warm enough. Actually, it is more on the hot side than on the warm. My thing likes it to be hot enough.

My pink thing is very tender. So I am careful. When I have the water flowing as I need it, I lie down on the bottom of the bathtub, and spread my legs apart bent in the knees. It is a sexy position. My pussy is eager to finish. It knows how sweet the feeling is. It knows how full the relaxation is because Diane does not have to worry to make a partner happy. Therefore, I can totally relax with myself.

I am by myself. Nobody is watching me. It is my gift of love to my beloved man. You are the first and the last in such a private session. I feel very happy about this detail.

My thing is pink and cute. It is waiting for the treat. I am holding the showerhead directing the water to my thing. It is very pleasant feeling. Absolutely pleasant. The water is fondling everything I want with even and persistently strong current. It softly hits the little cute soft hiding button on the top of the pussy, then it goes lower and it tenderly but persistently hits a beautiful entrance to the paradise that we both love to satisfy so much.

I am thinking of you. I am saying to myself, "Oh Baby, do me, lick me, stronger, more, please, how good you are licking me, how good you are, I am going to finish very soon. Lick me Baby, lick me more. It is your tongue so hot and tender, going all around my pussy. Do me, Baby, do me simultaneously with your beautiful hard tense cock. More! Harder, harder, harder, faster, faster, faster, while water is hitting me on the little button on the top. Do me, fuck me into the entrance of the pink paradise while water is fucking me on the top.

What an unearthly pleasure! I am flying in the skies, it is a paradise, I love it so much, I could do it over and over". That is what I think before I finish. Finishing comes usually rather quickly. It is very good and strong. Then, right away, comes the feeling of tiredness and sleep.

Of course, it is not as sweet as to make my beloved proud too, sharing the experience of loving each other together, but it is definitely good physical relaxation and rather innocent experience by itself.

I hope you liked it, my Baby.

Sometimes, I do it right away once more. Yes, sometimes I can do it two times in a row.

You know, you are my cute Baby.

How I love to share my intimate things with you! I have a secret hope that you can do yourself too when

reading   me.
Nevertheless, I want it to be our secret. I would never ask you about it. I know you are a shy man. However, in the depth of my soul I hope that may be you will do it to yourself too, to relax your tension and have that healthy nap afterwards. I know that you understand me

and appreciate my sharing with you. You are so smart, responsive, and very cool.

You are the coolest man I have ever known in my life.

I Love to Show My Weakness to You

I am very vulnerable, very pleasantly vulnerable. I love to show my weakness to you and to express it to you the way I can.

I am hugging you and kissing you on the lips, very tenderly. I am kissing you with a very deep and slow kiss going slowly with my tongue on your lips, on your tongue. Your tongue is hot and wet. It is moving together with my tongue. It is a very wet kiss. I am kissing you, and kissing you, and kissing you. I cannot have enough of you. I am drinking you as if an exhausted traveler in the desert drinks the water from the spring. And I am touching you everywhere inappropriately. Very inappropriately. It is so exciting - to touch you inappropriately. I am rubbing your jeans in the most inappropriate place. It feels warm, and hard, and live there. It feels very cute there. Very promising and responsive. Absolutely cute. You are fondling my breasts with your warm tanned hands. It is very pleasant. I am very excited. I want you with all my heart. I want to have you with my entire woman's soul.

I am taking your hand and you are helping me unzip your jeans. We are impatient like children who want their favorite toy. We want that hot and hard thing out. We both want it out very much. I want to work on that hard thing. I want to make you feel very good. I want you to be very happy and forget all your other thoughts except this very pleasant action with me.

Forget about everything, my Baby. Relax my Baby. I am fondling and caressing your tender, hard, hot thing. It is very cute and full of desire. I love you very much, my Baby. You know that I love you, don't you?

I am sliding lower between your legs and I am taking that thing into my mouth. It is very cute, very smooth, and very hot. It is so cute and wild with desire. I am taking it deep into the mouth wrapping my lips around the tender smooth thing. I am licking it and sucking it. Licking it and sucking it. I am pushing it inside and out, in and out, in a slow and pleasant motion. It goes so smoothly and slippery in and out, in and out. You love it, my Baby. You love it very much. You are very cute, because you love what I am doing to you.

You are doing me, and doing me and doing me. We both love it very much. It is very pleasant and exciting. We are very excited, we love to do you. You are my cute Baby, you are enjoying yourself very much. You love to do me. You can do me over and over, and I will never be tired to love you because it excites us both a lot.

You are fucking me, and fucking me, and fucking me, and you cannot have enough of it. I love to do you, my Baby. I am full of you. I love to be done by you.

The action is getting hotter. You want to finish. You push your thing harder, you go faster, and faster, and faster, very deep. It is so good, my Baby. It is the best thing to do when you are in love. It drives the both participants totally crazy. When I am writing this, my thing is squeezing in a pleasant feeling. I feel like you are going to finish. You are going to finish, my sweet Baby. Please fuck me, fuck me more, my Baby, fuck me faster, push your thing deeper; it is so delicious to fuck you, my Baby.

You are coming, my Baby. I feel that you are coming now, my Baby. Come my Baby, come my dear man. It is so good. You are finishing very strongly and a lot. I can hardly swallow it. I am sucking it, like an ice cream, to make your moment of pleasure longer. It is a piece of my cute Baby. It is a happy piece of him.

You are very happy, my beloved. We both are smiling.

What happiness is to be with you, being wrapped with the sea of pleasure, and forget about the world around!

I Can't Stand to Look at Your Jeans

We are in the car talking. I can't stand to look at your jeans as you are sitting here beside me. I know I should not do it here. But I want it very much. I am pretending I need to get something from that car pocket that is on the side where you are sitting right now, on the car door. So I am leaning over you, over your jeans, close to you, touching your jeans with my breasts, and I am pretending I need to get a notebook from that car pocket. I see that you are moving on the seat excitedly but you are shy to show your desire. Well, I am shy too. I love shy men! They are the best. They keep all their feelings of desire inside until you let them to get you, until you let them to get what they want from you.

I am now going to tell you what I would do if I could have now what I want.

I want to rub your jeans where that thing is and where legs are. I love men's legs. I love athletic legs, or long athletic legs. I love the shape of man's legs, of your legs, when you sit quietly, and I know inside you is rocking and rolling a storm of desire. You hardly can keep it. But you know that the best treat from me is when you hold it until I start insisting on getting you myself.

I am putting my hand on your thing, and I am sliding my hand along your legs. I love man's spread legs in jeans. It is such a turn on when you want that man. I love that very light man's perfume or shower gel aroma that comes from your clothes, from your skin. It attracts me physically, like a shark is attracted with the smell of blood even in a big distance.

I am fondling and fondling your thing through jeans. Then I slowly open your zipper. There is a warm wonderful thing inside. It is like a cute hard animal sitting there. Sitting quietly waiting for its turn. It knows its turn for pleasure is coming. It is almost here.

I am cautiously taking the top of the thing out of the captivity of the jeans. I start kissing the top of it. Very tenderly. My lips are wearing pink lipstick. I do not want to leave any traces of the lipstick on your clothes. I know I will not. I will eat all my lipstick in the process. I am kissing the head of your beautiful tight hard thing with my wet lips. My lipstick is already eaten by now. I am licking your cock and I am licking my lips with my tongue. Now I can take it deeper. I am playing with your cock kissing its head simultaneously. I am squeezing its body very tenderly with my warm, loving, and tender hand with light pink pearl enamel on my natural, not fake, not overly long, fingernails.

I think by now I am already sitting almost in front of you to be able to enjoy having your thing more conveniently.

I am sucking it. It is very nice. It is very delicious. I am going from up to down. I am sliding your thing into my open mouth very tenderly deeper and deeper. In and out. In and out. My lips are wrapped tight around your handsome cock. I am making delicious sounds as if I am eating a candy.

I am sucking on a candy. A slippery sweet milky chocolaty candy. I am going slowly at first. From top to the base, from top to the base. My tongue is very pink and tender. It loves sucking on a candy. It loves sucking your candy. I have been thinking about you all day. Now I am having my reward - you and your candy.

My breasts are in the pink lacy bra. They look very cute in the open unbuttoned top. I take your cock out of my mouth and push it between my breasts. We are enjoying each other very much.

Your cock is missing the mouth though. I know it. That is the plan. I took it for a moment between my breasts so it would be missing coming back to the mouth.

I am taking it to the mouth again. Now you are already so turned on, that you cannot bear it anymore, you want to fuck me hard, so you could explode. You want to explode on my breasts because they are so delicious and cute. No, you want to start exploding deep in the mouth, into the throat, but you also want to sprinkle your sperm on my beautiful pinky lacy breasts, so I could lick it out of there, too.

You are starting fucking me harder. You are fucking me in the mouth very good. I feel your huge desire. I feel your enormous pleasure and impatience to finish.

Oh, fuck me, fuck me baby, I love you very much. I want you to fuck me well. I want you to satisfy yourself fucking me very well. I want to give you that pleasure - again and again. I adore your constant desire. I know that you have been thinking about me all day, too. I know how you are sometimes doing yourself when I am not with you. I want to fuck you well, so you could enjoy it to the fullest with your woman.

Explode, explode my baby! Oh, I feel now how it is coming as an avalanche into my throat. You are moaning. I ask you to take it out and give it to my breasts. We got it now on the top of my lacy breasts. I am taking one of my breasts out of the bra licking your sperm from it. I can hardly reach it, but yet I can. It is cute.

It is cute to see it, and it is cute to do all of it.

You are saying that you love me so much that it was not enough for you, that you want to fuck me more. You know how I love you fucking me. That is why you are saying you want me more. You want me to get more of you.

You want to fuck me in the pussy.

I am wearing a narrow jeans skirt, tights, and leather boots. I am pulling up my skirt, then I am unzipping my boots - they are tall knee-high leather beige-brown boots with a zipper in the back. I am taking off one boot and the tights from one leg.

Now we see a very cute lacy pink bikini. You are kissing me through them, teasing the lacy pink pussy with your tender hot lips. I am impatiently taking the bikini off too, to better and sweeter enjoy your caresses.

Now we see a cute impatient pussy, pink and waiting for the sexy party. It is shaven with a narrow strip in the middle. The pussy lips are ready for your tongue. You kiss me in the pussy lips. But to do it here is not very comfortable. So I am softly pushing you aside and now I am sitting on you. I am going to ride you as a cowgirl.

I am fucking you so good and tender, and we are enjoying ourselves enormously. I am fucking you and fucking you, riding you and riding you. You are holding me with your tender hands at my waist and you are helping me to ride you better. I wish we could have room here to enter my pussy from behind! I love when you are doing me from behind. I love to turn around your cock. But in this little space we cannot do it. So we are continuing the riding motion.

I want you to kiss me. You are whispering, "Sit on me, my baby, I want to kiss your beautiful pussy, I want you to come too". I am an obedient woman. I like to obey my man. I am moving as you ask me. Now I am giving you my pink open-lips wet beautiful pussy to your mouth, to your lips. It is unbelievably pleasant. You are sucking on my pussy so tender and good. You know how I like it. Very tender and monotonous. You go on the top, then down, into the narrow wet tunnel of paradise. You are sticking your tender slippery tongue there. You are fucking me with your tongue. What unimaginable pleasure! My beloved! I am going to finish soon.

I am starting being tense, as I always do before exploding. My beloved, how good you are fucking me with your tongue! Here, I am coming... Eat me, eat me, my beloved, eat all of it! Now fuck me quickly, fuck me right away, I want to feel your hard warm cock inside me. Yes! Now I feel like

I am continuing exploding. More, more, my beloved. How good that I have you my Baby! What pleasure to fuck you, what pleasure to be fucked by you!

Thank you my beloved! I feel your final explosion inside me.

We are totally happy, and we can take a peaceful nap now

after hard work of loving each other.

www.ingramcontent.com/pod-product-compliance
Lightning Source LLC
Chambersburg PA
CBHW060201290526
45789CB00003B/1109